D0604868

J
364.3
HAN

*AMERICA'S MOST WANTED*

*Public Enemy Number One:*
# GEORGE "BABY FACE" NELSON

**Written by:**
**Sue L. Hamilton**

Published by Abdo & Daughters, 6537 Cecilia Circle, Bloomington, Minnesota 55435

Library bound edition distributed by Rockbottom Books, Pentagon Tower, P.O. Box 36036, Minneapolis, Minnesota 55435

Library of Congress Number: 89-084922                    ISBN: 0-939179-61-X

Cover Illustrated by: Liz Dodson
Inside Photos by: Bettmann Archive

# Edited by: John C. Hamilton

# FORWARD

**Saturday, March 3, 1934**

"I've got it all worked out,"said the 5'5" Lester
Gillis, better known as George Nelson. Strutting
up and down in his hotel room in St. Paul,
Minnesota, the baby-faced killer turned to look at
his latest companions. Master criminal John
Dillinger and two of his gang members, John
"Three-Fingered Jack" Hamilton and Homer Van
Meter, sat uncomfortably watching their newest
"leader."

Dillinger had just escaped from Crown Point Jail
in Indiana, making his way immediately to St.
Paul. His getaway from the "escape-proof" prison
had made headlines in all the newspapers. He was
the FBI's Public Enemy Number One — an honor
that Nelson wanted for himself. Many of Nelson's
bank jobs were thought to have been the work of
Dillinger, a twist of fate that Nelson hated. He
wanted everyone to know *he* was in charge. Quite
happily, he now had the mighty Dillinger working
for him.

*John Dillinger worked under the leadership of Baby Face Nelson.*

Smiling, Nelson said, "We'll hit the bank in Sioux Falls, South Dakota. All we gotta' do is blow in, blast anyone who gets in our way, and blow out with all the cash. It'll be so quick they won't know what hit 'em!"

The Dillinger gang sat momentarily in silence. Dillinger's usual method was to carefully scout a bank, find out when the biggest haul was in the vault, and get in and out without hurting anyone. But Nelson didn't believe in all that. He didn't care about anything but money. His way could easily get a lot of people killed. (Including the gang members!)

Van Meter had taken all he could from the short, crazy man. Suddenly, he burst out laughing. The "plan" was stupid and dangerous, Van Meter thought. It had to be a joke! But it wasn't to Nelson.

"Nobody laughs at me!" growled the killer. Grabbing his submachine gun, Nelson pointed it at Van Meter, his finger on the trigger.

"Wait," yelled Dillinger, leaping up and knocking the gun away. "We've got to work together," he said, towering several inches over Nelson. "Homer didn't mean nothin', did ya, Homer?"

Knowing how close he was to death, the seasoned bank robber swallowed his last chuckle before saying, in as serious a voice as he could muster, "No, I didn't mean nothin'. Sorry."

"OK," growled Nelson, still tensed, ready to lift his gun. "But nobody laughs at me."

"Let's get together tomorrow and go over everything," said Dillinger. "We've had enough for today."

**Sunday, March 4, 1934.**
Late the next day, Nelson and Dillinger set off in Nelson's car, headed for Van Meter's room. Plans were shaping up for hitting The Security National Bank in Sioux Falls, South Dakota. Dillinger had worked all day convincing Nelson to do things his way. Nelson was tired of listening to Dillinger. Who was in charge of this job, anyway? he thought.

*One of the many banks Baby Face Nelson robbed.*

"Look, it's my job," said Nelson angrily, taking his eyes off the road to stare at Dillinger. "Let's just get in and out with the cash. Fast and quick. That's the way I do..."

"Look out!" yelled Dillinger.

With a loud crash of grinding metal and broken glass, Nelson plowed into the rear of another car.

Inside the other vehicle, 35-year-old Theodore C. Kidder turned to his wife and her mother. "Are you all right?" he asked.

"Yes, we're OK," said Mrs. Kidder, "But I think the car is damaged."

"Well, this guy who hit me is going to pay for everything!" said Kidder, getting out of his car and running over to Nelson's vehicle.

"Are you blind?" shouted Kidder, leaning into the driver's side. "You had a stop sign..."

Without wasting a second, the already-angered Nelson picked up his .45 pistol and pressed the trigger. Kidder's face was only inches away. The bullet hit him right between the eyes, killing the young paint salesman instantly. As the body slumped to the ground, Nelson backed up his car and roared away before anyone could stop him.

Shocked, Dillinger asked, "Did you have to do that?"

"Yes!" Nelson yelled. "He recognized *you*!"

"Well, a citizen got your license number back there," responded Dillinger angrily.

Swearing and pounding the steering wheel, Nelson drove like a madman out of town. Dillinger sat quietly, glancing at the gun lying in Nelson's lap. Once again, Baby Face Nelson had proved himself the maniac killer that everyone knew he was. Dillinger didn't want to be his next victim.

## CHAPTER 1 — BABY FACE'S EARLY YEARS

Life was tough from the beginning for Lester Gillis. Born December 6, 1908, he lived with the stinking smell of rotting meat near the Chicago stockyards. With little education, he soon joined the hoodlums roaming the streets. However, his small size was a constant disadvantage, making him the source of jokes and joy of bullies.

He grew up knowing that one day he'd be "somebody." To him that meant becoming the toughest, meanest man anywhere.

In his early teens, he decided the first thing he had to do was change his name. Calling it "too sissy," he became George Nelson, and tried to get everyone to call him "Big George." Of course, his short height and sweet blue-eyed face made that nickname silly. Behind his back, he was always known as "Baby Face" Nelson — an alias no one ever said to his face. He knew about it, though. He hated it, and he would kill anyone who used it around him.

His first arrest came at the age of 14. For stealing a car, he was sentenced to two years in a boys' home. Receiving a parole in 1924, he hit the streets once again. For the next several years, he found himself in and out of jail. Stealing was one racket. His other trade was "heist and protection." He would go into businesses, hold them up, take their money and leave. Later, he would return and ask the owners to pay him for protection against himself!

In 1928, while deep in the crime world, Nelson met a young woman in a Chicago Woolworth's store. She smiled at the cute Nelson. Short and pretty, Helen Wawzynak would soon become his wife.

The following year, Nelson went to work for Chicago's king of crime, Al Capone. At the young age of 21, Nelson was hired to get payments from labor unions. Unions, groups of people who joined together to make their jobs better, were easy pickings. Each month people would pay dues, and it was Nelson's job to collect Capone's share. If a union leader wouldn't pay, Nelson was suppose to beat him up. Sometimes, however, Nelson would do his job a little too well, and he'd end up killing the guy instead of just hurting him.

Within two years, Nelson was without work. Never knowing what the killer would do, the crime bosses simply stopped using him for any jobs. Nelson turned once more to robbery. On January 15, 1931, he held up a Chicago jewelry store. Arrested several days later, the judge gave Nelson a sentence of one year to life. Nelson became Inmate #5437 in the "Big House," the state prison in Joliet, Illinois.

*The infamous mob leader from Chicago, Al Capone.*

On February 17 of the following year, Nelson escaped from prison, never to be caught alive again. The crazed killer was loose, and he meant to become the greatest criminal in the world.

## CHAPTER 2 — THE BIG TIME

After escaping from prison in Illinois, Nelson headed for California. While things quieted down in the Midwest, he worked for Joe Parente, a bootlegger who made his money buying and selling illegal liquor.

As he bided his time, Nelson met up with John Paul Chase. Not too smart, but very loyal, Chase became Nelson's most trusted companion, and first gang member.

In 1932, Nelson and Chase headed for Long Beach, Indiana, a popular gathering place for criminals. Tommy Carroll, well known for his skilled use with a machine gun, joined Nelson's gang. Next came Eddie Green, a "jugmarker" — someone who scouts out banks, choosing which one to hit next.

*George "Baby Face" Nelson.*

The gang did well, stealing from banks in Iowa, Nebraska, and Wisconsin, but Nelson was angry that credit for his jobs was going to John Dillinger. He wanted everyone to know that he and his gang were behind those holdups. However, Dillinger was the top man in 1933, the FBI's Most Wanted, so rather than try to beat him, Nelson tried to join him.

"Do you need another gun?" asked Nelson to Dillinger's right-hand man, Homer Van Meter. Van Meter replied, "We don't know you, Nelson. And we don't trust you."

Nelson left, more determined than ever to show-up the well-known Dillinger. His chance came in February 1934. Dillinger was about to break out of prison. However, little was left of Dillinger's "Super Gang" — most were in jail or dead. Only Van Meter and John Hamilton were left on the outside. Nelson had a gang and jobs lined up.

Van Meter and Hamilton set up a meeting with the pint-sized criminal. Awkwardly, Van Meter began, "Johnny's breaking out of that tin can soon. Do you have any big action for us?"

More powerful than he'd ever been before, Nelson was enjoying the uncomfortable situation Dillinger's henchmen were now in. They needed him. He didn't necessarily need them. But how could he turn away such experienced help? Pausing, the bank robber replied slowly, "Yeah, Eddie Green has marked two jugs in Sioux Falls, South Dakota, and Mason City, Iowa. Big dough there."

He squinted at the two henchmen and asked the most important question, "Can Dillinger take orders?"

"Why you little..." said Hamilton angrily, moving towards Nelson.

"They're my men and my jobs," said Nelson with cold fury in his voice. Even Hamilton knew what little it took before Nelson would reach for his gun. Hamilton paused.

Quickly, Van Meter jumped in. "Johnny will go along with it," he said. What choice did they have? he thought. Right now they needed money, and they needed the crazy "Baby Face" to help them get it.

# CHAPTER 3 — TAKING CHARGE

On March 3, 1934, Dillinger had indeed made his escape from Crown Point prison in Indiana. Meeting with Van Meter and Hamilton, he discovered what awaited him now that he was free.

"Nelson has some jobs lined up," said Van Meter.

"I'd probably be better off in the joint than joined up with that madman," said Dillinger.

"You haven't heard the worst," said Hamilton.

Van Meter said quietly, "The guy thinks he's in charge. He wants to order you and us around."

Dillinger sat quietly. "We've got to get some money. If he's got some jobs, I'll go along with it. But watch him. The guy doesn't think twice about blowing someone away."

*Inside the Sioux Falls bank where Baby Face Nelson murdered one of his several victims.*

18

Dillinger's statement came true the following day when Nelson, a bad driver to begin with, plowed into a car driven by Theodore Kidder. Nelson didn't care about blowing away some innocent man in front of his wife and mother-in-law; Nelson was angry. The guy got what he deserved. He was in the way. The only trouble was, now the law might be after them. Heading towards South Dakota, Nelson just kept driving — fast and furiously.

As luck would have it, no one knew for sure who had killed Kidder. Nelson got away with it...temporarily.

On March 6, Nelson led Dillinger, Hamilton, Van Meter, Green, and Carroll into The Security National Bank of Sioux Falls. Still angrily trying to outdo Dillinger, the maniac went crazy when a teller set off a security alarm.

Over the piercing blare of the alarm, Nelson screamed shrilly, "I'm going to kill whoever hit that alarm!"

Ignoring him, Dillinger pushed Van Meter and Green towards the cash drawers. Quickly, the three gathered the money.

Nelson continued screaming. Suddenly, he saw a movement by the window. As if hunting game, the maniac leaped over a railing and flung himself on a desk, blasting off four quick shots through the nearby window. Outside, an off-duty cop fell dead, never knowing what had happened.

"Let's get out of here!" said Dillinger, moving towards the door.

"I got one of them! I got one of them!" sang Nelson, happily.

Taking over, Dillinger ordered several hostages out to the car. Safely protected by the terrified bodies of those unfortunate enough to be in the bank, the car sped away, leaving a trail of nails on the road behind to slow down anyone following them. Once they had gotten away, Dillinger let his captives go unharmed.

Nelson counted out the money as though nothing had gone wrong. Nearly $50,000! He had really done a good job. Dillinger, however, couldn't believe he was working with the baby-faced maniac.

# CHAPTER 4 — AGAINST THE FBI

A week later, the robbers hit the The First National Bank of Mason City, Iowa. Again, Nelson went crazy, wounding the bank's vice-president, and aiming to finish him off. Only through Dillinger's help was the man left alive to report that the gangsters had made off with $52,000.

Dillinger knew they were in trouble. Police were alerted all across the Midwest. They needed to lay low. With his own cut of the loot, each gangster headed in a different direction.

After several weeks, Dillinger called everyone together. Hamilton, Van Meter, Carroll, and Nelson met up in a quiet resort known as "Little Bohemia" in northern Wisconsin. Late in the evening of April 22, 1934, the gangsters had no way of knowing the FBI had surrounded the lodge.

Suddenly, the shooting began. Everyone but Nelson followed Dillinger out the back of the main lodge, across an escape route that Dillinger had mapped out earlier. From a nearby cabin, apart from the others, the pint-sized gangster held two pistols in his hands. Preparing to make his break, Nelson opened the cabin door, aimed carefully, and blasted a shot right passed FBI Agent Melvin Purvis, the man in charge of the capture.

Agent Purvis turned excitedly, pressing the trigger of his own Thompson machine gun. It jammed. Throwing it to the ground, he grabbed his .38 Special and fired at Nelson's fleeing form. Purvis raced after Nelson, and for a few brief moments the two traded shots in the dark. However, Nelson quickly blended into the inky blackness of the woods, leaving Purvis to return to his men and lead the assault on the now-emptied lodge.

Crazed and alone, Nelson stumbled through the woods. Finally, he fell into a clearing. Ahead of him lay Koerner's Resort. Gun in hand, the dirtied, wild-eyed killer burst in on the Koerners

*FBI agent · Melvin Purvis.*

and Emil Wanatka, the owner of the Little Bohemia Lodge. Wanatka had just arrived, having raced through the woods to get help when shots were fired at his resort.

"I want a car. Now!" screamed the enraged Nelson. "Now, or you're all dead!"

Forcing Koerner and Wanatka outside, Nelson jabbed his pistol into Wanatka's ribs and said, "Start the car."

Still breathless, Wanatka sat and turned the key. A low grind met Nelson's ears. The car wouldn't start. "Get it started," yelled Nelson wildly. "Or you're both dead!"

Again, Wanatka tried. The car still wouldn't start. Suddenly, the sound of another car's engine added to the chorus. Agents J.C. Newman and W. Carter Baum, along with Carl C. Christiansen, a deputy from nearby Spider Lake, roared into the yard. Sent by Purvis to make a phone call, the policemen were met by a short man pointing two .45's directly at them.

"Get out," said Nelson, wildly gesturing with the pistols. As the three prepared to get out of the car, Nelson yelled grimly, "I know you wear bullet-

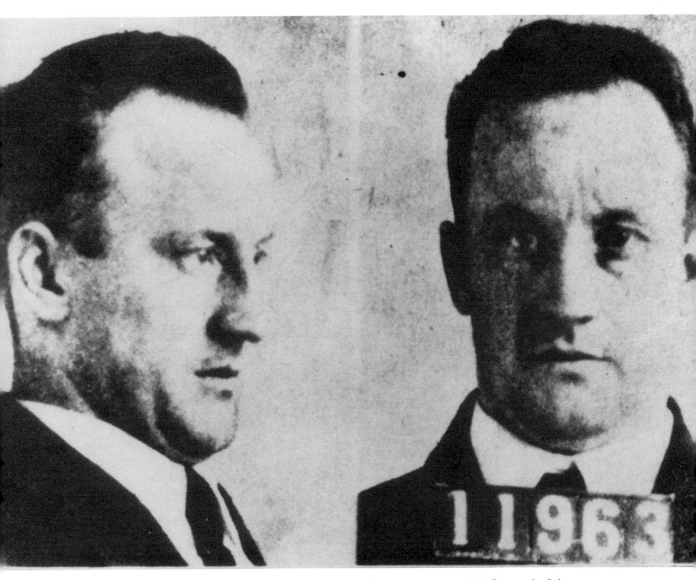

*Wanted for murder, bank robberies and prison escape - $100 Reward - John Hamilton. John Hamilton was Nelson's partner in crime.*

proof vests, so I'll give it to you high and low."
With that, he opened fire. Baum was killed
instantly. Christiansen was blasted off the running
board on the opposite side of the car, while
Newman was shot where he stood.

Without a backwards glance, the killer leaped into
the FBI agents' Ford and roared away. While
Dillinger and the others had beat a safe retreat,
never firing a shot, the insane Nelson had
managed to terrorize several people, wound two
men, and kill one. Still, he'd gotten away, and that
was all that mattered to him.

## CHAPTER 5 — THE LAST SHOWDOWN

On July 22, 1934, something happened that
changed Nelson's life. John Dillinger was killed by
the FBI in Chicago. Nelson was now on top:
Public Enemy Number One.

Heading back to California to lay low for awhile,
the killer met up with his friend, John Paul Chase.
"It's not right," said Nelson. "Dillinger wasn't any

better than me, but the price on his head was a lot more than mine." With a wicked grin, Nelson continued, "But I'm going to fix that. I'm going back to the Midwest and give them something to remember!"

But how? Aside from his wife, Helen, and John Chase, Nelson had no more gang. Tommy Carroll had been killed in a gunfight in Waterloo, Iowa. G-men caught up with Eddie Green in St. Paul, Minnesota. He was now dead. Hamilton had been wounded after the Little Bohemia raid, and died days later. Homer Van Meter had been double-crossed and gunned down on August 23, 1934. Still, Nelson wanted to make his mark, and returned to the Midwest in September 1934.

But nobody wanted anything to do with him. "Die," was the underworld's response. Nelson would shortly fulfill that command.

On November 27, 1934, FBI Agents Sam Cowley and Herman Hollis spotted Nelson's car on a country road near Fox River Grove, Illinois. Nelson raced off, blasting his gun wildly behind him. Cowley and Hollis followed, returning fire.

*FBI agent - Herman Hollis.*

Just outside Barrington, Illinois, Nelson stopped the car, letting his wife out to hide in a nearby field. Right behind, the FBI agents stopped and got out. Cowley dropped into a nearby ditch. Hollis braced himself against the back of their car.

Suddenly, the air filled with the blasts of machine guns. Nearby highway construction workers fell to the ground, watching the unbelievable scene unfold.

Several minutes passed. The ground was littered with spent bullet shells. Finally, Nelson had enough. As though he believed himself invincible, the madman stood up and said to his friend Chase, "I'm going over there and get them!"

Like an Old West gunfighter, Nelson slung his machine gun low on his hip and walked slowly across the road towards the two FBI agents, firing round after round.

Amazed, Cowley paused only a moment, then opened fired at his target. Nelson took several hits, but kept walking. Finally, just steps away,

Nelson stopped, looked directly into Cowley's eyes, and fired. The blasts nearly cut the agent in half. He died instantly.

Nelson now turned his attention to Hollis. The G-man shot several rounds, blasting bullets into Nelson's legs. Still, the pint-sized killer kept coming. "Come on, you yellow-belly...! Come and get it," screamed Nelson. His shotgun empty, Hollis ran for cover behind a telephone pole and drew his pistol. Grinning wickedly, the baby-faced murderer walked forward as Hollis emptied his gun into him. Pressing the trigger in a long burst, Nelson cut Hollis down, just as he'd done to the G-man's partner.

Silence filled the country road once again. Nelson turned and walked towards the G-men's car, staggering the last two steps. Chase and Helen raced up to him, and all three piled in. "You'll have to drive," said Nelson to Chase. "I'm hit."

# EPILOGUE

The following day, a naked body with *17* bullets in it was found in a ditch near Niles, Illinois, about 20 miles away from the standoff. How the killer had survived so many hits will never be known. Chase had stripped Nelson to keep the police from finding out who he was. However, it didn't take long to determine the body's true identity.

A month later, Chase was captured and sentenced to life in prison. Helen Gillis was also captured and spent a year in a women's prison in Madison, Wisconsin. After serving her time, she was released, and was never heard from again.

As for Nelson, he finally got his wish. At the age of 26, he became one of the most famous killer/bank robbers of the 1930's. The country would not soon forget him, nor would the FBI. Still, in a mocking twist of fate, his most hated nickname would stick with him, for instead of "Big George" Nelson, he will always be remembered as "Baby Face."

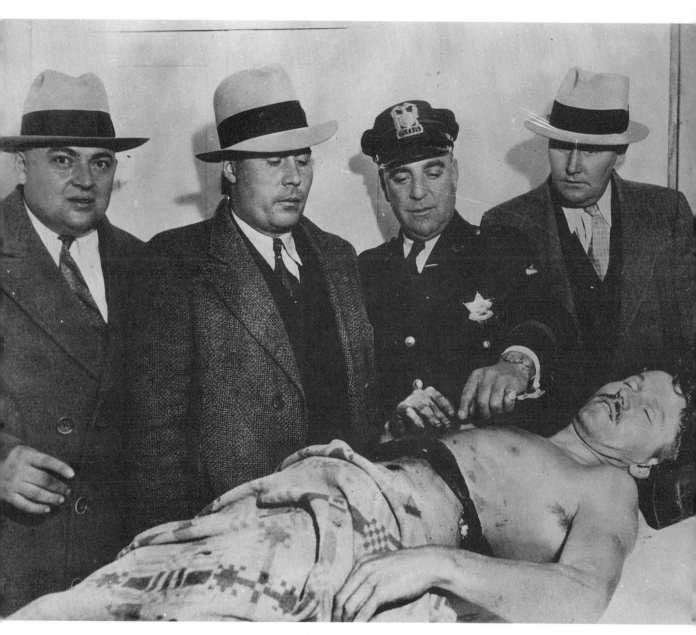

*George "Baby Face" Nelson finally got what he wanted, to be a Public Enemy #1, America's most wanted criminal.*